S0-BIN-117

Turn

Turn

Christopher Patchel

Turn Turn

ISBN 978-1-936848-14-0

Book design and illustrations
Christopher Patchel

Cover armillary sundial
<Photos.com>

Red Moon Press
PO Box 2461
Winchester, VA
22604-1661 USA
<redmoonpress.com>

rmp

turn

are turning

have been turning

have turned

will turn

will be turning

will have been turning

will have turned

turned

were turning

had been turning

had turned

Preface

A quick study I'm not. In putting together this overdue collection it took several years of musing on my decade of published haiku to fully recognize the theme of time that runs through my writing. Time in all its manifest forms and hues: The *chronos* progression and duration we mark off with clock and calendar. And *kairos* experiences only the heart can measure, whether of new love, a pink slip, the smell of honeysuckle, or slant of light… occurrences that arrest our attention, awaken a sense of *carpe diem*, or even intersect eternity "At the still point of the turning world." *(T. S. Eliot)*

Haiku traditionally tends to be time-oriented, of course. Focusing on ephemeral singularities against the backdrop of perennial seasons is a prime way such brief poems gain resonance and meaning. Which could well be the long and short of the time motif in my own work. Or it may be the other way around, that I was drawn to haiku as a way to work out my place in the order of things, a pursuit given new wind in midlife.

Whatever the reasons for whatever my fascinations, haiku continues to be a satisfying medium for exploring the essence of things. And sharing my finds with my fellow inhabitants of time continues to be the most gratifying part.

Christopher Patchel
Mettawa, IL
June, 2012 A.D.

Acknowledgements

Since I first became aware of it at the turn of the millennium, the haiku community—local, national, international—has been invaluable as a source of inspiration, education and camaraderie. Likewise, I am very grateful for the support of fellow artists and writers in my *Lively Arts* group over the years, as well as other friends and family who let me pester them for their opinions.

Nearly all the poems in this collection previously appeared in the following journals, sometimes in slightly altered form: *Acorn, Bottle Rockets, Contemporary Haibun, Frogpond, Haijinx, Haiku Light, The Heron's Nest, A Hundred Gourds, Mainichi Daily News, Mayfly, Modern Haiku, Presence, Raw Nervz, Reeds, Simply Haiku, Still.*

A number of poems received awards in contests: *The Haiku Calendar Competition 2002, 2005, 2006, 2007, 2009, 2010, 2011, HaikuNow! 2011, Harold G. Henderson Award 2011, Midwest Poetry Review Contest 2001, Penumbra 2001, 2002.*

And many of the poems were also republished in these anthologies: *Breath of Surrender, Haiku 21, Magnapoets Anthology 1 and 2, Montage, A New Resonance 3: Emerging Voices in English-Language Haiku, Per Diem, Red Moon Anthology of English-Language Haiku 2001–2011, Seed Packets.*

To the editors of all the publications mentioned, my sincere appreciation.

Turn Turn

To everything there is a season,
and a time for every purpose under heaven.

Ecclesiastes 3:1

As Long as I Like

Forever is composed of nows.

Emily Dickinson

one year older
the softness
of spruce tips

start of summer
I inch myself
into the water

supermarket
the cart with a child
at the prow

school's out
boys get a trucker
to blow his horn

freeway
a hand on the wheel
a hand in the wind

fireflies
and I get to stay out
as long as I like

the long day
a bug
cleans its antennae

deep night sky
the car radio
between stations

from the big bang to my funny bone

midnight stars
a walk through the neighborhood
trips light after light

day moon
the only living boy
in Chicago

skip of the heart a shooting star

tall grass
both teams lose track
of the score

Olympic Games
a record time
in my Lazyboy

summer twilight
the walking path dips
into coolness

katydid chorus
nothing that can’t wait
until tomorrow

thrush song
the play of light
on my eyelids

end of summer
the ice cream jingle's
doppler shift

September
on the wall calendar
post-it notes rustling

the clamor
of unseen sparrows
a yellow maple

how I linger
at the summit…
autumn colors

slant light…
to each leaf
its own fall

catching a maple leaf
just before the ground—
Indian summer

starlings leave
the leafless trees
the silence

blank space
where the calendar hangs—
New Year's

morning fog…
the blinking
of my cursor

graffiti
under and over
a layer of white

long evening
a different silence
in each room

horn
of a freight train bordering on
dream

morning snowscape
the whistling
of dove's wings

winter blues
the gnaw of my boots
on old snow

a hot shower…
finding the note
that resonates

first person singular breath plumes

pillow turned
to the cool side—
spring morning

daylight saving time…
wearing my jacket
with the liner out

first spring day
even out of doors
I want to go out

March wind
enough already
with the excuses

study break
I can’t stop bursting
the bubblewrap

meadow breeze
so little depends upon
white butterflies

form 1040 due—
blossoming cherry,
magnolia, pear

scent of lilacs
and a sudden fancy
to rhyme

plum blossoms…
we don't define
the relationship

Kindle and Dim

Lord, keep my memory green.

Charles Dickens

one year older
the smell of honeysuckle
after the rain

hometown
the hug
of the hills

a radio oldie
from childhood…
the double entendres

midafternoon…
faint caws
from a far-off summer

First Love

She was a horticulture major. A girl-next-door type with unstyled blond hair and bitten nails who went braless and wore hiking boots. She drove a green Volkswagen Beetle and was nicknamed Itty for her own petite size, which she more than made up for with energy and heart. We shared nature outings, rock concerts, church services, brushes with the law. While at separate colleges she wrote long letters and often made the four hour drive to visit me. What more did I want.

a wicker basket
once filled
with wildflowers

the niece
I cradle in my arms
wants down

the same hilltop
but on the other side
of summer

if onlys
what ifs—
twilight

start of autumn
I dream I'm a latecomer
and only half dressed

must it be the rattle of acorns

leaf fall
I get her to do
the talking

a shadow
and its butterfly
fall equinox

in final descent
to the airport
dusk

at a loss for words a lunar eclipse

crabapples…
the neighbor and I
compare ailments

debating politics at a potluck dinner

our reminiscing…
the late-night clocks
turned back an hour

Retrospect

victory celebration
a navyman
kissing a nurse

children huddled
to their migrant mother
in a lean-to

how many college boys
does it take
to fill a phone booth?

one protester
versus
a column of tanks

the grainy blur
of a soldier's
D-day landing

an audience
of straight faces
in 3D glasses

flashbulb bursts
Marilyn's
billowing white dress

stark naked
fleeing
the burning napalm

firefighters
raising a flag
over ground zero

moonscape
the dark and light sides
of earth

used books
I leave the shop
an hour older

a path of leaves
our conversation
turns wordless

autumn dusk
I mutter
to myself

memories…
the leaf pile embers
kindle and dim

first snow…
back under
the covers

settling creaks
of the cottage timbers
winter dusk

wetting my thread
for the eye of the needle
winter solstice

longest night
the strains of carolers
come and gone

checkout line
faces of celebrities
no longer with us

night train
we are all in this
alone

partly sunny New Year's morning

writer's block
I clean out
the refrigerator

January
my new car's
first scratch

midwinter thaw
the prize claim notice
in a sweepstake

continued cold
another revision
of my resume

I double check
my stack of mail
hunger moon

in like a lion—
the buds
of a pussywillow

the sigh
I heave…
forsythia

blossoms
my envy
of lovers

spring woods
the quick
and the dead

spring cleaning—
what does and doesn't
wash off

blossom rain…
but you hope we can
still be friends

You Are Here

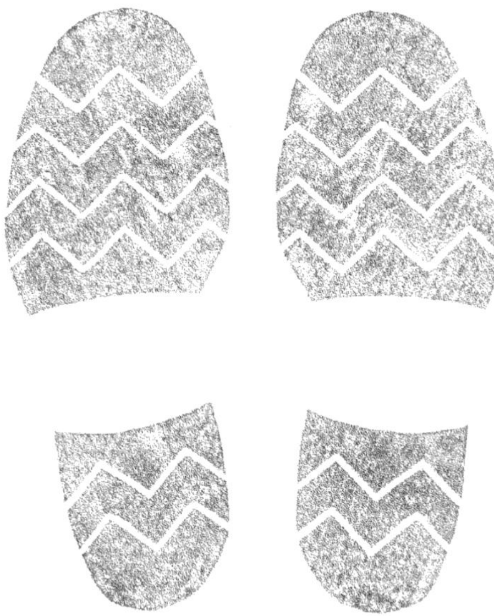

December is the toughest month of the year.
Others are July, January, September, April, November,
May, March, June, October, August and February.

Mark Twain

another birthday
worn soles
on my dance shoes

colonoscopy—
pushing it back
another month

midlife
my car radio
on scan

dog days
the ice cream jingle
a four-measure loop

butterfly...
one day
at a time

summer's end
the weight of my body
out of the water

ready or not goldenrod

blue asters
God grant me
the serenity

burning bush
maybe there's still
hope for me

city life
I missed
my exit

nightly news
then
the north star

my Chicago
streetmap
separating
into ribbons

aerial photograph
my house
with its skylight

Home

I count fifteen addresses that I called home for a time, the last eight of them since moving here to Chicago. There was the upstairs flat with roaches, three shared houses, two noisy apartment buildings, the high-rise, and now a tumbly cottage. My lease renewal is coming up. I wonder if I'll stay or not.

milkweed puffs…
too old to be loading
a moving truck

midfall…
having dreams that my car
doesn't brake

Clarity

closed concession stand rhythm of the surf

for all is vanity more leaves at the door

autumn clarity counting floaters in my eyes

the presence of the moon in another haiku

twilight starlings horizon to horizon

a lone hoot through the hollow

long night
internet friends
of internet friends

crowded mall…
the fountain's
wishing coins

a bank notice
of insufficient funds
winter solstice

year's end
well-worn pages
of the psalms

fortune unchanged
I reuse
the wall calendar

the new year…
I dream
of Sisyphus

fingers set
on the home keys—
my resolutions

north wind
the holes
in my beliefs

below zero…
verbalizing
my self talk

black ice less certain than I sound

You Are Here
the crisscross
of snow flurries

dead of winter…
relighting
the pilot flame

writer's block
the return key
won't

snowed in all Groundhog Day

mud month
the long wait
for a tow truck

Perennial

While I breathe I hope.

Latin Proverb

the chorus
before the cranes
spring sky

perennial...
the garden
I dream of

we turn turn our clocks ahead

one year older
the joy
of skipping a stone

nameless longings
a floating seed
eludes my hand

Christopher Patchel was born late spring on the East Coast, the sunrise side, Eastern Daylight Time, and grew up in rural Pennsylvania, a short distance from the Atlantic.

One leaf-turning autumn in midlife he moved to the Midwest, Central Standard Time, to do publishing design in lakeside Chicago.

Someday, he'd like to live on Pacific Time, and spend in his sunset years along the warm shores of the West Coast.

a full sail
the sea and sky
one blue